EXPLORE

The World of
WEATHER

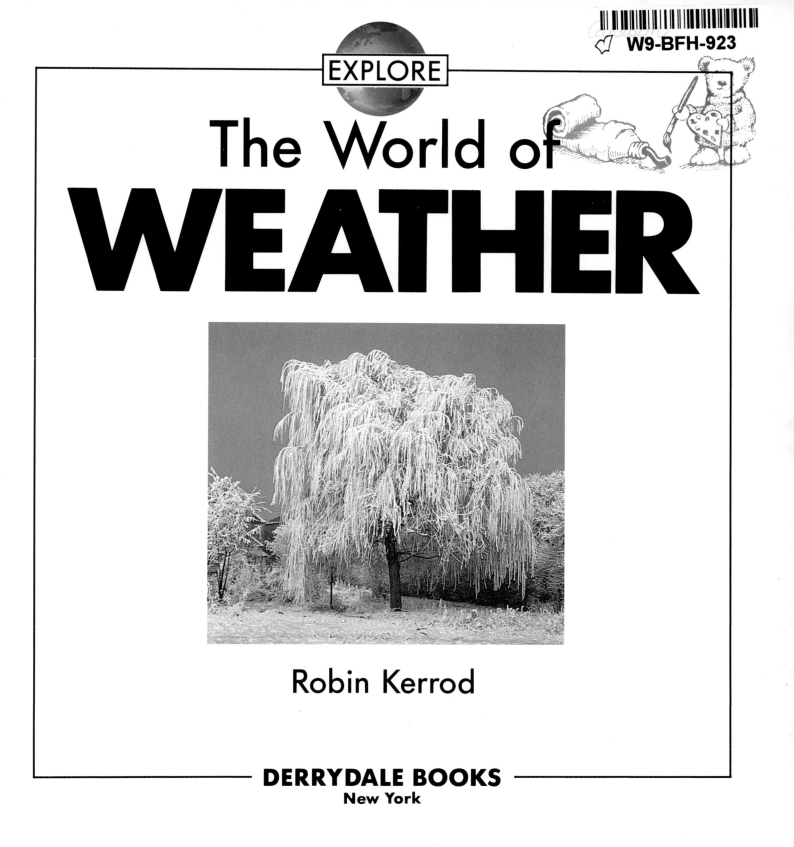

Robin Kerrod

DERRYDALE BOOKS
New York

A SALAMANDER BOOK

First published by Salamander Books Ltd.,
129-137 York Way, London N7 9LG,
United Kingdom.

© Salamander Books Ltd. 1991

ISBN 0-517-05910-X

8 7 6 5 4 3 2 1

This 1991 edition published by Derrydale Books, distributed by
Outlet Book Company, Inc., 225 Park Avenue South,
New York, New York 10003.

Printed and bound in Belgium.

CREDITS

Designed by: John Strange

Artwork by: Mike Saunders

Color separation by: P & W Graphics, Pte. Ltd., Singapore

Printed by: Proost International Book Production, Turnhout,
Belgium

CONTENTS

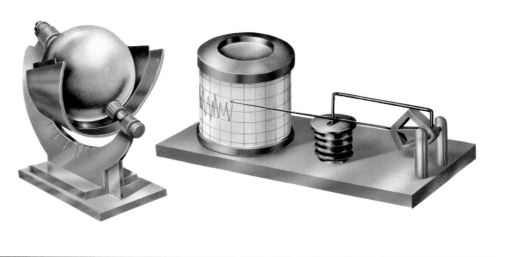

WHAT'S THE WEATHER LIKE?

People throughout the world ask this question every day. It is not surprising, because the weather affects us all. For example, it affects how we dress, how we get about and how we spend our leisure time. We can't wear a T-shirt

▲ A magnificent sunset. A vivid red evening sky like this is supposed to be a sign of fine weather next day.

and shorts on a frosty day, cycle to school in thick fog, or play ball in a thunderstorm.

The weather affects some people in particular, such as farmers. For example, their crops can be ruined and their livestock killed by flooding,

◀ A dried-up lake in Ethiopia, Africa. Little rain has fallen there in recent years, causing all the crops to fail.

caused by too much rain; or by drought, caused by too little. For other people, the state of the weather can be a matter of life and death. Black ice on winter roads can cause cars to slither and crash. Violent storms at sea can sink ships.

But what exactly is weather? We can think of it as the conditions that exist in the air about us at any time. This includes the temperature and pressure, and the amount of moisture the air holds. Other features of the weather include winds, clouds, rain, snow, hail, fog and frost.

We call the science that deals with the weather, meteorology, and the scientists who study it, meteorologists. By studying past and present weather, they try to predict, or forecast, what the weather will be like in the future.

In this book we look at the many different aspects of the weather. We examine what drives the weather systems (the Sun); how they move (the winds); and the forms of precipitation they bring (rain, snow, and so on). We follow meteorologists as they go about their work.

We also look at the many different weather patterns, or climates, found throughout the world.

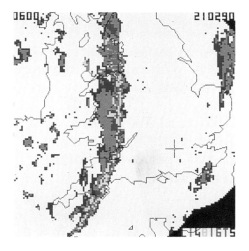

▲ **This computer image shows rain falling along a weather front. Computers are widely used in forecasting.**

▶ **Cloud patterns in a blue sky. Studying the clouds is a good way of telling what the weather is going to be like.**

7

THE SUN AND THE EARTH

◄ How astronauts view the spinning Earth from space. The continent is Africa.

The main cause of the weather is the Sun. It provides the energy for the weather machine. It pours out into space enormous amounts of energy as light and heat. Only a tiny fraction of this reaches the Earth.

The Seasons

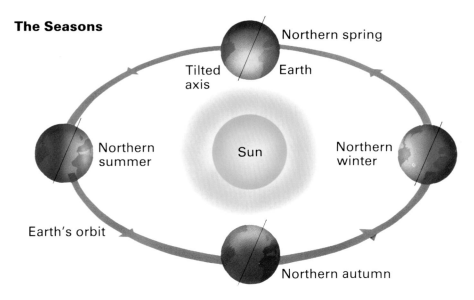

▲ The four seasons. In spring and autumn the Earth's axis is tilted neither towards nor away from the Sun.

But the energy that does reach the Earth is enough to raise the temperature in some places to more than 120°F (50°C); to drive winds at speeds of over 200 mph (320km/h); and to evaporate (turn into gas) millions upon millions of gallons of water from the oceans every day.

Temperature, wind and the evaporation of water are key features of the weather. Temperature is by far the most important feature. Winds arise mainly because of differences in temperature between different parts of the Earth. Water evaporates more on hot days than on cold days.

Different Weathers

People in different parts of the Earth experience different kinds of weather. For example, in places near the Equator, the weather is always hot and rainy. On the other hand, at the North and South Poles, the weather is always very cold and snowy. Elsewhere, the weather is not so hot nor so cold. It may rain or snow, or it may not.

In other words the kind of weather you get depends on where you live. This is because the Sun's rays fall on different parts of the Earth at different angles.

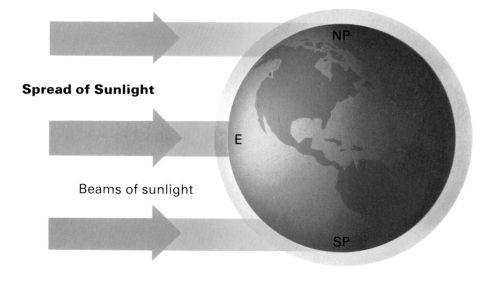

Spread of Sunlight

Beams of sunlight

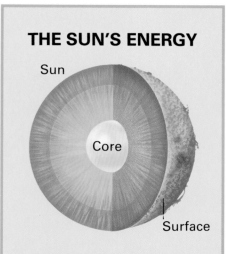

THE SUN'S ENERGY

Sun

Core

Surface

The Sun is made up mainly of very hot hydrogen gas. This gas acts as fuel in the nuclear fusion process that produces the Sun's heat. In the process the nuclei (centres) of hydrogen atoms fuse (join up) to make a new gas, called helium. Fantastic energy is given out.

▲ **A beam of sunlight spreads over a smaller area at the Equator (E) than at the North and South Poles (NP, SP).**

Spinning And Tilting

The Earth travels in a circle around the Sun once a year. As it does so, it spins like a top on its axis, which is an imaginary line through the North and South Poles. If the Earth's axis were upright in space, the temperature in a certain place would stay the same throughout the year.

But in fact the Earth's axis is slightly tilted. So as the Earth circles the Sun, a place is sometimes tilted towards and sometimes away from the Sun. The more it is tilted towards the Sun, the more heat it receives and the hotter it is. This explains why in most parts of the world the temperature and weather change throughout the year.

The Seasons

We call the regular changes in the weather pattern during the year the seasons. In many parts of the Earth there are four seasons: summer, autumn, winter and spring.

In the Earth's Northern Hemisphere, midsummer is on June 21. That is when it is tilted most towards the Sun and receives most heat. Midwinter is on December 21, when the Northern Hemisphere is tilted most away from the Sun.

In the Southern Hemisphere, the seasons are the other way round, with midsummer in December and midwinter in June.

FACT FILE

● The Earth's axis is tilted at an angle of 23½ degrees.
● The Sun measures about 865,000 miles (1,400,000km) across.
● At the time of the equinoxes (March 21 and September 23), there are 12 hours of daylight and 12 hours of darkness all over the world. The word 'equinox' means equal nights.

THE ATMOSPHERE

We live at the bottom of a great ocean of air, which we call the atmosphere. It stretches from the ground up to a height of over 300 miles (500km). The air is thickest, or most dense, near the ground because it is squashed by the weight of the air above. It becomes thinner, the higher you climb above sea level. Eventually the atmosphere fades away to nothing, and then you are in space.

The air in the atmosphere presses down on us and everything else on Earth. At sea level it presses down on every square inch with a force

▼ **In orbit we see clearly the thin layer of atmosphere. Beneath it we see the oceans and above it, black space.**

of 14.7 pounds (1kg on every square centimetre). We say that the atmospheric pressure is 14.7 pounds per square inch (1kg/sq cm).

As you climb higher and the air thins out, the atmospheric pressure falls rapidly. At a height of 10 miles (16km), the pressure is only about one-tenth that at sea level.

Layers Of Atmosphere

We can divide up the atmosphere into layers. The bottom layer, where the air is thickest, is called the troposphere. This is where most of our weather occurs. It varies in depth from about 5 miles (8km) at the North and South Poles to about 12 miles (18km) at the Equator.

Above the troposphere lies

OTHER ATMOSPHERES

The Earth is one of nine planets that circle in space around the Sun. Except for Mercury, all the other planets have an atmosphere.

Mars has only a thin atmosphere, made up mainly of carbon dioxide. This gas also makes up Venus's thick atmosphere, in which the pressure is 100 times that on Earth and the temperature is an oven-like 900°F (480°C).

The giant planets Jupiter, Saturn, Uranus and Neptune each have a very deep atmosphere. It is made up mainly of hydrogen gas, with a little helium and methane. The picture shows the Great Dark Spot in Neptune's atmosphere.

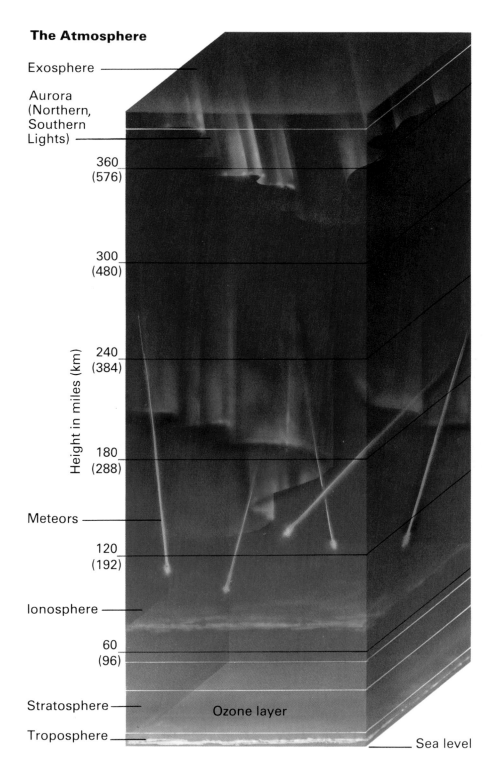

The Atmosphere

- Exosphere
- Aurora (Northern, Southern Lights)
- 360 (576)
- 300 (480)

Height in miles (km)

- 240 (384)
- 180 (288)
- Meteors
- 120 (192)
- Ionosphere
- 60 (96)
- Stratosphere
- Troposphere

Ozone layer

Sea level

the stratosphere, which extends up to about 50 miles (80km) high. Within this region is a layer of ozone gas. The ozone layer is very important because it blocks most of the Sun's dangerous ultraviolet rays. These are the rays that burn our skin when we go out in the Sun.

In The Ionosphere

Above the stratosphere is a deep layer called the ionosphere. Here there is hardly any air left at all. The little air left exists in the form of ions, or electrically charged atoms. That is what gives this layer its name. It is the ionosphere that makes possible round-the-world broadcasting, because it reflects radio waves. In the lower part of the ionosphere, the fiery streaks we call meteors become visible.

The ionosphere extends to a height of about 400 miles (650km). Then comes the final layer of atmosphere, called the exosphere. Scarcely any traces of air now remain, and gradually the atmosphere merges into space.

◀ **A section of the Earth's atmosphere. Our weather takes place in the troposphere, the lowest and thickest layer.**

AIR AND SKY

▲ Cattle graze under a blue sky. The air provides gases to protect and keep alive all living things on Earth.

The atmosphere around us plays many parts, not only in the weather, but also in keeping us alive. It helps keep us warm like a blanket by holding in the Sun's heat. It filters, or takes out, dangerous rays from sunlight. And, in particular, it enables us and all other living things to breathe.

The air in the atmosphere is made up of a mixture of gases. The most important one is oxygen. This is the gas we, and all living things, must breathe to stay alive. Oxygen makes up about 21 per cent (about one-fifth) of the air by volume. The rest is mostly nitrogen gas.

There are also small amounts of carbon dioxide in the air. Living things give off this gas when they breathe out. Green plants use carbon dioxide from the air to make their food. They combine it with water, which they take in through their roots, to make sugar. The energy they need comes from sunlight. This food-making process is called photosynthesis.

The amount of carbon dioxide in the air is steadily increasing, mainly because of the fuels we burn. This increase is leading to global warming, and is threatening to change the world's weather and climate (see page 44).

Another gas is present in

▶ **How much oxygen is in air? Find out in this experiment. Water rises in the jar because the oxygen is used up.**

▼ **At sunset the sky sometimes turns red. The colour comes about because dust in the air only lets through red light.**

1 Place a lighted candle in a bowl.

2 Pour in some water.

3 Place a jar on top.

4 Candle goes out when no oxygen is left.

the air in tiny quantities. It is the gas we call water vapour, formed when liquid water evaporates. The movement of air masses containing water vapour around the globe is one of the main factors that affects the weather.

The Sky

The sky is the atmosphere as we see it from the ground. It is like a great bowl over our heads. The sky is changing all the time. It often gives us a good idea of what the weather is going to be like in the near future. A clear blue sky is the best sign.

But why is the sky usually blue? Air itself is colourless. The answer lies in the nature of sunlight. It appears white but is in fact made up of a mixture of light of many colours – the colours which

we see in the rainbow. When sunlight passes through the air, the air particles scatter blue light into our eyes more than they scatter other colours. And so the sky appears blue.

FEATURES OF THE WEATHER

As already mentioned, there are three key features of the weather. They are the air temperature, the air pressure, and the amount of water that evaporates from the oceans into the air. We call the amount of water vapour in the air, the humidity.

When any of these features changes, we can be sure that other weather conditions will change too. A change in the air pressure, for example, may signal a change in the speed and direction of the wind. A change in the humidity may mean that rain or snow is on the way.

That is why meteorologists measure temperature, pressure and humidity at regular intervals. This helps them prepare their weather forecasts (see page 34).

▼ Instruments for measuring the weather. Many people have thermometers and aneroid barometers at home.

▼ **This Masai woman lives in Africa. Her dark skin helps protect her from the sunshine.**

Weather Instruments

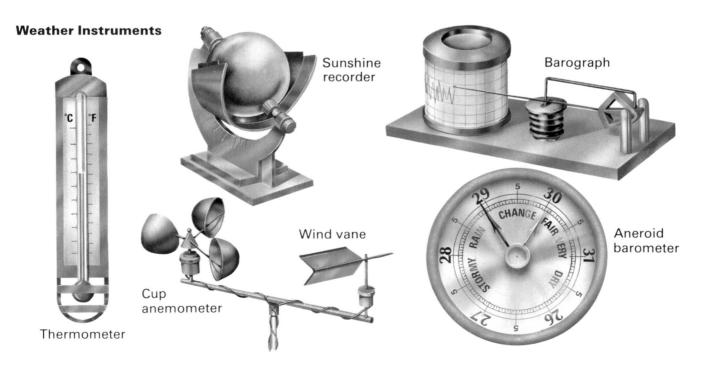

Thermometer

Cup anemometer

Sunshine recorder

Wind vane

Barograph

Aneroid barometer

14

Temperature

Meteorologists measure the temperature of the air with thermometers. These indicate the temperature by the height of a column of liquid in a narrow tube. The liquid metal mercury and coloured alcohol are often used. When the temperature rises, the column of liquid rises. When the temperature falls, the column of liquid falls.

Thermometers measure temperature in degrees on the Fahrenheit scale (°F) or Celsius scale (°C). On these temperature scales, water freezes at 32°F and 0°C; and boils at 212°F and 100°C.

Pressure

Pressure is measured with a barometer, or a barograph, an instrument that makes a record on paper with a pen. Some barometers contain a device which gets smaller as the pressure goes up and bigger as the pressure goes down. This movement is a measure of the pressure.

Weather scientists measure pressure in a unit called the bar. The average pressure of the atmosphere at sea level is about 1 bar. But usually pressures are given in millibars (mb), or thousandths of a bar.

Rising air pressure is often

▼ This scientist is taking a reading from a hygrometer at a weather station. The instrument measures humidity.

◀ Mist hangs over a river in the early morning. Soon the mist will disappear as the Sun's heat turns it to vapour.

a sign that better weather is on the way. Falling pressure often means that unsettled and rainy weather is coming.

Humidity

Humidity is measured by instruments called hygrometers. One kind of hygrometer uses a long hair. It works because the length of our hair changes when the humidity changes.

THE WIND

The air about us is always moving, making wind. In general, winds blow because of differences in air pressure between one region and another. They blow from regions of high pressure to regions of low pressure, always trying to even out the pressure differences.

In turn, the differences in pressure over the Earth are usually caused by differences in temperature. Where the surface is warm, the air above heats up. It expands, becomes lighter and rises. This sets up a region of low pressure. The surrounding colder air is now at higher pressure and moves in: a wind springs up.

Reversing Winds

Small-scale winds spring up at the seaside in the summer. During the day a breeze blows in from the sea, and during the night it blows in the opposite direction. These breezes spring up because of differences in temperature between the water and land.

A similar reversing wind pattern occurs on a much larger scale in India during

◄ This tree has been blown by the prevailing wind all its life. That is why is has become permanently bent.

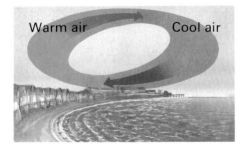

Warm air   Cool air

◄ On hot days at the seaside, the land gets hotter than the water. The air above it rises, causing a breeze to blow in.

► At night the land cools more than the water. Air rises above the water, and causes a breeze to blow out to sea.

Cool air   Warm air

16

THE BEAUFORT SCALE

Devised by Francis Beaufort in 1806 to estimate wind speeds.
The scale ranges from wind force 0 to wind force 12.

No.	Name of wind	Wind speed		Effects of wind
		mph	km/h	
0	Calm	0-1	0-1	Smoke goes straight up
1	Light air	1-3	1-5	Smoke slightly bent
2	Light breeze	4-7	6-11	Leaves rustle
3	Gentle breeze	8-12	12-19	Leaves move
4	Moderate breeze	13-18	20-29	Small branches move
5	Fresh breeze	19-24	30-38	Small trees sway
6	Strong breeze	25-31	39-49	Large branches move
7	Moderate gale	32-38	50-60	Whole trees sway
8	Fresh gale	39-46	61-74	Twigs break off
9	Strong gale	47-54	75-86	Roofs damaged
10	Whole gale	55-63	87-100	Trees uprooted
11	Storm	64-75	101-120	Widespread damage
12	Hurricane	Over 75	Over 120	Wholesale destruction

FACT FILE

● The summer monsoons in India often bring torrential rain: as much as 30 ft (9m) of rain may fall in a month.
● A wind belt called the jet stream circles the Earth at high altitudes; flowing from west to east, it travels at an average speed of about 125 mph (200km/h), but sometimes reaches double this speed.

winter and summer. In the winter, the wind blows from the cold land out to the warmer sea. In the summer, the wind blows from the sea on to the much hotter land. These seasonal winds are called monsoons. The summer monsoons are wet and bring with them heavy rain.

In many parts of the world the winds blow from the same direction most of the year. For example, in North America and Europe the winds generally blow in from the west. Farther south, the

▲ Hang-glider pilots can stay aloft longer if they can find air currents moving upwards.

winds usually blow in from the east.

We call such winds prevailing winds. They arise mainly because of the difference in temperature between the Equator and other parts of the world.

Speed And Direction

The wind varies in speed and direction from day to day. Meteorologists measure wind speed with a rotating cup device called an anemometer. In storms, winds may blow at speeds of over 100 mph (160km/h).

Wind direction is measured with a wind vane. Winds are always named after the direction from which they blow: for example, an east wind blows from the east.

WHIRLING WINDS

On very hot days in summer, you sometimes see little whirling columns of leaves and dust rise above dusty ground. We call them dust devils. They are a kind of whirlwind.

Dust devils form when air is heated by the hot ground and rises quickly, picking up dust. They never grow very tall and last for only a few minutes.

► **A tornado on the move in Oklahoma, USA. The wind has spiralled down to the ground from the storm cloud.**

They are harmless and cause no damage. However, other whirlwinds, called tornadoes, are terrifying and cause enormous damage.

Terrifying Tornadoes

Tornadoes can spring up in many parts of the world, but are most common in the United States. There, 500 or more tornadoes occur every

◄ **This is the kind of damage a tornado does when it passes through a built-up area. The houses are blasted apart.**

year. Tornadoes measure about 330 ft (100m) across and can travel for hundreds of miles before they blow themselves out.

A tornado forms at the bottom of a towering black thundercloud, and then spirals its way down to the ground. It is a kind of funnel,

JUPITER'S SPOTS

Furious whirling winds are found on other planets besides the Earth, including Jupiter, Saturn and Neptune.

On Jupiter the winds have created storms so big that astronomers on Earth can see them through their telescopes. One is shown in the picture above. Another is called the Great Red Spot because of its colour. It is oval in shape, and measures about 17,500 miles (28,000km) long and 8,750 miles (14,000km) wide.

▲ **A dust devil springs up from the hot dusty ground. Large ones can lift small animals like rabbits into the air.**

formed by winds rotating at speeds of 300 mph (500km/h) or more. Inside the funnel, the air pressure is very, very low. If the tornado passes through a town, houses in its path literally explode as the air inside suddenly expands.

Whirlwinds can sometimes occur at sea: we call them waterspouts. Their funnels of wind suck up columns of water. Waterspouts occur most often in tropical oceans. They do not last long and cause little damage.

Much larger whirlwind

systems also form in tropical oceans. They can cause great destruction and loss of life. When they form in the Atlantic, they are called hurricanes; in the Far East, they are called cyclones, typhoons or willy-willies.

A hurricane is an area of rotating winds, measuring up to 375 miles (600km) across. The winds spiral around the centre at speeds of up to 190 mph (300km/h). But in the centre there is a calm region (the 'eye') about 22 miles (35km) across.

The winds pick up lots of moisture as they pass over the water and dump it as torrential rain. They also whip up the waves, which add to the destruction when the hurricane hits the coast.

▼ **Space shuttle astronauts spied this great cyclone over the Indian Ocean. It measured hundreds of miles across.**

19

THE WATER CYCLE

'The Earth' is, perhaps, not a good name for our planet. We really ought to call it 'The Water', because water covers more than 70 per cent of its surface.

The water does not stay put in the oceans. Every day a lot of it 'disappears'. This happens because it changes into a gas and enters the air. We call this gas water vapour.

The presence of water vapour in the air has a marked effect on the weather.

The water does not stay in the air for long as vapour. It soon becomes liquid again and

▼ **The water cycle never ends. Water enters the air as vapour from the land and sea, and leaves it as rain and snow.**

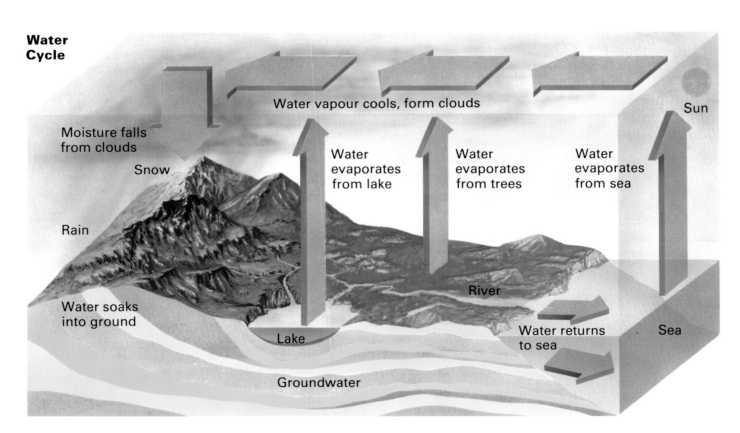

Water Cycle

Water vapour cools, form clouds

Sun

Moisture falls from clouds

Snow

Water evaporates from lake

Water evaporates from trees

Water evaporates from sea

Rain

River

Water soaks into ground

Water returns to sea

Sea

Lake

Groundwater

▼ Mist hangs over a lake in Sweden. Both the water and the evergreen trees are giving off vapour into the air.

► A spider's web sparkles with dewdrops. Dewdrops form when water vapour condenses on surfaces on cool nights.

falls back to the surface. The circulation of water between the surface and the atmosphere is never-ending, and is called the water cycle.

Round The Cycle

Let us follow water in the oceans around the cycle. The Sun heats up the surface water and causes it to evaporate, or turn into vapour. The vapour rises into the air and begins to cool. As it cools, it turns back into tiny droplets of liquid water. The droplets gather together to form clouds.

Within the clouds, the water droplets collide and form bigger and bigger drops. In time the drops become heavy enough to fall to the ground as rain. If the temperature is low, the drops may freeze and fall as snow. On the ground, the rainwater or melted snow runs off into the rivers, and in time back into the oceans. The cycle begins again.

From The Land

Water also circulates between the atmosphere and land areas as well. It evaporates from rivers, lakes and the soil. It is also given off by trees and other plants.

When plants make food in their leaves, they use water, which they take in from the soil through their roots. But they take in much more water than they need. They give off the rest as vapour. This process, called transpiration, plays an important part in the water cycle.

Mist And Fog

When moist air cools near the ground, a kind of cloud often forms there. We call such a cloud a mist if it is thin, or a fog if it is thick. Mists and fogs often form on very still autumn nights when the air cools rapidly.

In industrial regions, smoke and fumes may get trapped in fog, and cause a choking, smoky fog we call smog. Smogs are very unhealthy.

CLOUDS

We can tell a lot about the weather by looking at the clouds. In summer we often see little puffs of white cloud move lazily across the sky, like sailing ships in a sea breeze. These clouds tell us that the weather will stay fine. We call them cumulus.

But sometimes these clouds swell up and darken, forming the shape of a blacksmith's anvil. Then we know that a thunderstorm is on its way, with loud claps of thunder, dazzling flashes of lightning and heavy rain. We call the thundercloud, cumulonimbus.

Cumulus clouds form at heights over about 5,000 ft (1,500m). Other clouds form even lower. They are called

FACT FILE

• The three main levels of clouds are low (up to 1.25 miles, 2km), medium-high (1.25-5 miles, 2-7km); and high (5-8 miles, 7-13km).
• The three basic cloud forms are cirrus (feather), cumulus (heap) and stratus (layer).

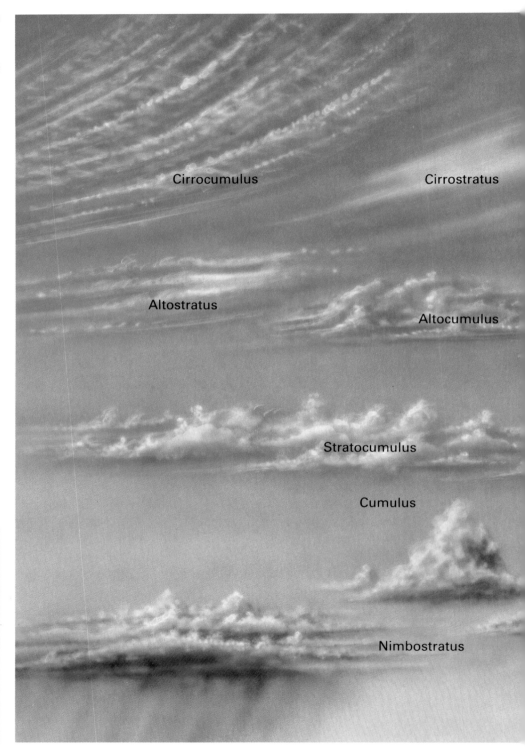

Cirrocumulus

Cirrostratus

Altostratus

Altocumulus

Stratocumulus

Cumulus

Nimbostratus

Cirrus

Cumulonimbus

stratus, or layer, clouds because they form a flat grey sheet all across the sky. They usually bring rain, or snow if the air is very cold.

In hilly regions stratus cloud often reaches the ground. If you walk into such a cloud, you find that it is made up of a fine wet mist. Cumulus clouds are like this too.

A Cloud Is Born

Low clouds are born when moist air near the ground is heated. This makes it lighter, and so it rises. As it rises, it expands and gets cooler. However, the cooler the air gets, the less moisture it can hold. And so the moisture condenses, or comes out of the air, as tiny droplets of water. These form a cloud.

Sometimes the air rises 4 miles (about 6km) or more. At such heights the temperature is below freezing. Then the moisture comes out of the air as tiny specks of ice. The clouds that form are often thin and wispy. We call them cirrus, or mares' tails. Another high cloud formation is cirrocumulus. We call it a mackeral sky because it looks like the pattern on the back of the mackeral fish.

◄ **(Main picture) Some of the main kinds of heap, layer and feather clouds that appear in the sky. You won't see them all at the same time.**

◄ **(Inset picture) A beautiful cumulonimbus thundercloud. Its broad, anvil-shaped top rises many kilometres high.**

23

RAIN

Rain is the most common form of precipitation (deposit) from the atmosphere. It consists of water drops up to about 0.2 inches (5mm) across. The heaviest rain falls in the tropics, where 5 ft (1.5m) can fall in a day. In some deserts no rain at all may fall in some years.

The rain that falls in the tropics is called convectional rain. It forms when strong convection currents of warm, moist air rise from the hot ground. As the air rises, it

FACT FILE

● Around a low, or depression, the winds blow in a circle: they blow in an anticlockwise direction in the Northern Hemisphere, and clockwise in the Southern. Depressions generally bring rainy, unsettled weather.

● Around a high, or anticyclone, the winds circle clockwise in the Northern Hemisphere, and anticlockwise in the Southern. Highs generally bring fine, settled weather.

▲ A tropical rain forest in Malaysia, South-east Asia, after a heavy downpour. The air is hot and steamy.

▼ Rain falls along both the cold and warm fronts in a depression. The cold air forces the warm air to rise.

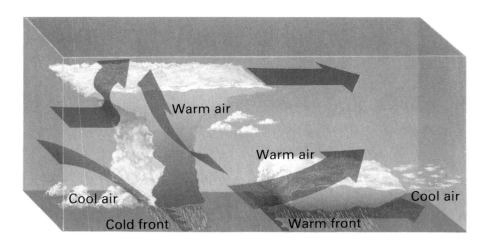

Warm air

Warm air

Cool air

Cool air

Cold front

Warm front

cools, and its water vapour condenses. Clouds of water droplets form. As they bump into one another, they form bigger and bigger drops, which soon become heavy enough to fall as rain.

Icy Rain

Convectional rain also falls on warm days in cooler climates. But there the clouds that form are much colder. They are made up of ice crystals high up and supercooled water droplets lower down. (Supercooled water is water that stays liquid even though the temperature is below freezing.)

In the clouds the droplets of

supercooled water swirl about and freeze as soon as they touch an ice crystal. The crystals grow in size until they are heavy enough to fall. When they reach the warmer air beneath the cloud, they melt and become raindrops.

Mountain Rains

Another kind of rain falls on mountains in coastal regions. It is called orographic rain. Warm, moist air blowing in from the sea rises up the mountain. Clouds form and rain falls, but mainly on the windward side.

◀ Here in Brazil, the River Piracicaba has burst its banks after heavy rain and has caused widespread flooding.

The air passing over to the leeward, or far, side of the mountain is now much drier. And so little, if any, rain falls there. It is known as a rain shadow area.

Depressions

Another type of rain occurs around areas of low pressure, known as lows, depressions, or cyclones. It is called cyclonic rain. It falls when warm air is forced to rise by cool air pushing underneath. It falls at the boundaries, or fronts, between the masses of warm and cold air.

◀ A rainbow forms when sunlight passes through raindrops and is split up into its many colours.

THUNDER AND LIGHTNING

Thunderstorms are the most spectacular of all weather happenings. They are great natural firework displays. During the storms, brilliant streaks of lightning zigzag

Thunderstorms occur almost every day in regions around the Equator, which are hot and humid. They also occur in temperate regions, but mainly in summer.

water drops and ice specks pick up electric charges. The water drops (negative charge) settle near the bottom of the cloud, and the ice specks (positive charge) near the top. Soon a very high voltage, or electric 'pressure', builds up in the cloud: it builds up to tens of millions of volts. (The electricity we use at home works at only 240 volts!)

◄ A vivid display of lightning in the night sky. It looks beautiful but can be deadly.

between the clouds and down to the Earth. Deafening claps of thunder rend the air.

Torrential rain and often hail lash down during thunderstorms. Icy hailstones cause a lot of damage to crops and may even kill people. Lightning starts forest fires, knocks down trees and buildings, and kills hundreds of people every year.

Charging Up

Thunderstorms are born when fluffy cumulus clouds start to grow into the huge dark clouds we call cumulonimbus. Within the growing storm cloud, air currents race furiously up and down. They carry with them little drops of water and specks of ice.

As they race about, the

FACT FILE

● During a hailstorm in Bangladesh in 1986, huge hailstones weighing up to 2½ pounds (1kg) killed more than 90 people.
● You can work out roughly how far a thunderstorm is away. Count the number of seconds between when you see the lightning flash and when you hear the thunder, and divide by 5. This gives the distance to the storm in miles. (Dividing by 3 gives the distance in kilometres.)

Electric Lightning

The electrical pressure in the cloud eventually becomes so great that the electricity begins to discharge, or leak away. An electric pulse called a leader makes a path through the air to conduct, or pass on, the electricity down to the ground or across to another cloud.

When the path is complete, a powerful burst of electricity races along it, creating a gigantic electric spark. We see this spark as a brilliant lightning flash.

The lightning stroke heats the air in its path white-hot. The air expands rapidly, creating a violent shock wave. This wave reaches our ears as a thunderclap. Because sound travels much slower than light, we always hear the thunder several seconds after

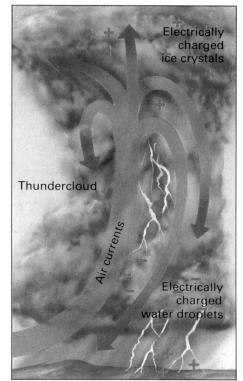

Electrically charged ice crystals

Thundercloud

Air currents

Electrically charged water droplets

▲ **In a towering thundercloud, violent air currents swirl about the masses of water drops and ice crystals.**

we see the lightning.

The lightning takes a zigzag path through the air, giving what we call forked lightning. Sheet lightning is a broad flash we see when lightning is reflected by the clouds. Ball lightning is much rarer. It looks like a fiery ball, which wanders hither and thither as though it has a mind of its own. It has even been known to chase people!

LIGHTNING CONDUCTOR

Lightning often strikes and damages tall buildings. But they can be protected by a metal rod called a lightning conductor, which leads down to the ground. When lightning strikes, the electricity can pass easily and harmlessly along the lightning conductor.

Lightning conductors are also used to protect other tall structures. The picture shows one on top of the space shuttle launch pad. The American statesman Benjamin Franklin invented the lightning conductor in about 1760.

27

SNOW AND FROST

JACK FROST

On freezing nights in winter, beautiful feathery patterns of ice crystals often form on the windowpanes. In fairy tales they are said to be the handiwork of a sprite called Jack Frost.

In fact the crystals form when water vapour in the air changes directly into ice when it touches the cold glass. This kind of frost is called hoar frost. The frost on the tree in the picture is called rime. It formed in freezing fog when the tiny water droplets in the fog instantly froze on the branches. Spring frosts can kill many young plants.

Snow is another common form of precipitation. It can fall at any time of the year in polar regions. But elsewhere it falls mostly in the winter.

It may be surprising, but the polar regions do not have the heaviest snowfalls. This is because the air there is fairly dry. The snow that has fallen over the years in Antarctica, around the South Pole, has packed down to form a massive ice sheet.

The heaviest snowfalls occur in mountainous regions in mid-latitudes, such as the Alps in Europe and the Rocky Mountains in the United States. In these regions as much as 10 ft (3m) of snow can fall in a year.

Snow is made up of tiny crystals of ice stuck together. Under a microscope, you can see that they are very beautiful. Each one looks like a six-pointed star.

Snow forms in the upper part of clouds, where the temperature is below freezing. When a cluster of crystals is heavy enough, it falls down

▼ **Drifting snow has blocked this road to traffic. Only the tip of a 10 ft (3m) high roadside fence can be seen.**

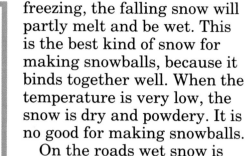

SNOWFLAKES

These are just three of the millions of snowflake shapes. Amazingly, each snowflake looks different from every other. The picture shown below is a photograph.

freezing, the falling snow will partly melt and be wet. This is the best kind of snow for making snowballs, because it binds together well. When the temperature is very low, the snow is dry and powdery. It is no good for making snowballs.

On the roads wet snow is the worst kind because vehicles pack it down to form sheets of slippery ice. Dry snow does not pack down so easily. Other snow hazards are heavy snowstorms, or blizzards, and drifting snow.

through the cloud. If the air temperature is above freezing, the clusters will melt and become raindrops. But if the temperature is below freezing, the clusters will fall as snow.

Sometimes snow and rain fall together, as sleet.

Wet And Dry
If the temperature at ground level is only just about

▲ Dog sleds are an enjoyable way of getting around in the snow. Traditionally, huskies are used for the dog team. They are strong, with great stamina.

WEATHER STATIONS

Almost all of us want to know what the weather is going to be like, to help us plan our work and play. To learn about the coming weather, we read the weather forecasts in the newspapers or watch them on the television.

The forecasts have been prepared by meteorologists. The first step they take in forecasting future weather is to gather information about the present weather. They

▼ Meteorologists feed data from weather stations into computers. These can show how the weather is changing.

▼ You can make a rain gauge yourself, with a jar and funnel of the same width. Sink your gauge into the ground.

▼ Try weather forecasting with seaweed and pine cones. Open cones mean fine weather; damp seaweed means rain.

Rain gauge
Funnel
Jar
Rainwater

Pine cone

Seaweed

gather this information from many sources: weather stations, space satellites, ships at sea and unmanned recording platforms.

Recording The Weather

Meteorologists take readings of weather conditions with a variety of instruments (see page 14). These instruments include thermometers and thermographs (to measure temperature), barometers and

▶ **This computer image shows in colour heavy rain falling along a weather front. The rain has been detected by radar.**

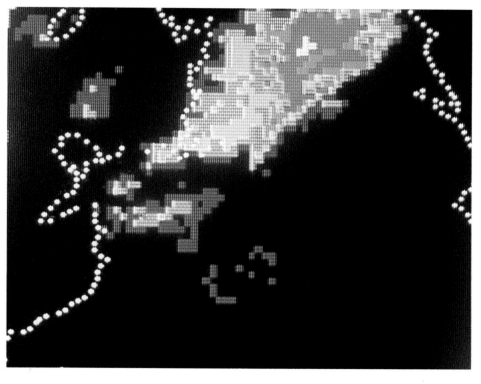

barographs (air pressure), hygrometers (humidity), anemometers (wind speed), wind vanes (wind direction) and rain gauges (rainfall).

Weather scientists also gather data (information) about other aspects of the weather, such as cloud cover.

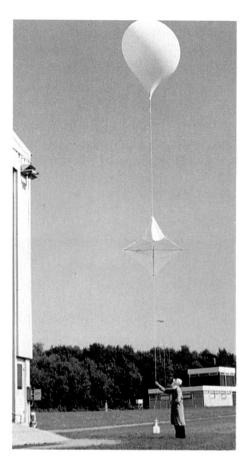

Coded Messages

The weather stations send the data they collect to national centres in the form of a code. The code consists of sets of five figures, such as 03772 81720 25231 08345 ...

In the code, the first group identifies the station, in this case London Airport (772), Britain (03). The second group indicates that the weather is cloudy (8) and that the wind is blowing at 170 degrees from the north. The last figures indicate the speed (20).

◀ **Launching a radiosonde. This weather balloon carries instruments high into the air and radios back readings.**

The Global Link

Weather knows no frontiers. And so meteorologists need to know what conditions are like, not only in their own country but worldwide.

Each national weather centre feeds its readings into an international information network. This is operated by the World Meteorological Organization, which is based in Geneva. The WMO then makes all the weather data available to meteorologists throughout the world.

31

WEATHER SATELLITES

▲ An American Delta rocket blasts off at Cape Canaveral, Florida, USA, carrying a NOAA weather satellite.

Altogether in the world there are about 9,000 main weather stations and many thousands of minor ones. These stations cover mainly land areas. Only a few stations report on the oceans. This is unfortunate because the oceans cover over two-thirds of the Earth's surface. And most weather systems are born in the middle of the oceans.

To watch the weather in the oceans, meteorologists turn to space technology. They send their measuring instruments into space on satellites so they can spy on the weather from above.

The United States launched the first weather satellite in 1960, called TIROS 1. TIROS (Television and Infrared Observation Satellite) took pictures of the Earth by day in visible light, and at night in infrared light.

Satellite Instruments

Today's weather satellites also carry similar kinds of instruments. The pictures they take in daylight show the pattern of clouds over the Earth, because they reflect sunlight. The infrared pictures they take during the night record the heat given out by the Earth. Clouds show up because they are cold.

Weather satellites carry a number of other instruments as well. These include microwave devices that can see through the clouds. They can take measurements of weather conditions at many different levels in the atmosphere. Satellites also collect data from unmanned weather platforms in remote parts of the world.

▼ A Meteosat weather satellite took this picture of Europe and Africa. It scans the Earth from geostationary orbit.

▼ A NOAA satellite picture of the United States. It shows most of the country clear, but cloud is building in the east.

Satellites And Orbits

Weather satellites circle the Earth in two main kinds of orbits, or paths. Some circle over the Poles, in a polar orbit. The American NOAA satellites, for example, travel in this orbit, while the Earth spins beneath them. They circle in orbit about 550 miles (850km) high and travel once around the Earth in about 1½ hours. They scan the whole Earth every 12 hours.

Other satellites circle high above the Equator. They travel at a height of about 22,300 miles (35,900km). In this orbit they circle around the Earth once every 24 hours. But the Earth itself turns on its axis once in this time too. So from the Earth these satellites appear to be fixed in the sky.

We call them geostationary (Earth-fixed) satellites. They take pictures of the whole hemisphere, or disc, of the Earth every half an hour.

NOAA Weather Satellite

Solar panel
(to produce electricity)

Instrument unit

Radio antenna

Instrument unit

▲ One of the latest NOAA satellites. The large solar panel produces electricity to power the instruments.

33

WEATHER FORECASTING

Every hour of the day and night, information about the world's weather floods into the World Meteorological Organization (WMO). It forms a vast information store, or databank. Meteorologists use this data to prepare the weather maps and forecasts we see in the newspapers and on the television.

Synoptic Charts

The first map meteorologists draw is called a synoptic chart. It gives a synopsis, or

► **A TV weather presenter ready to broadcast. His forecast will be based on the latest possible information.**

▼ **A series of newspaper weather maps showing how the weather in the Atlantic changes over three days.**

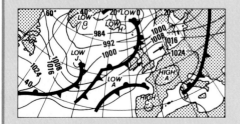

▼ **Fronts race from North America towards Europe, following the direction of the prevailing westerly winds.**

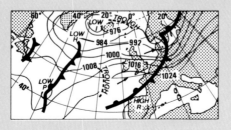

▼ **A frontal system, born two days ago, has reached Britain. Isobars are close together, indicating strong winds.**

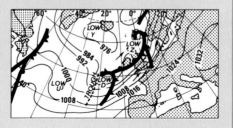

summary, of the existing state of the weather.

On a synoptic chart the position of each reporting station is marked with a circle. Around the circle the weather readings are written either in figures or symbols in standard positions.

After all the readings have been plotted, lines called

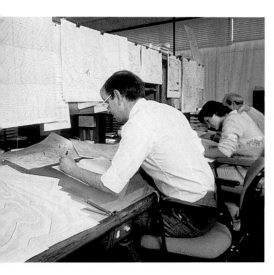

▼ At weather centres, meteorologists spend much of their time plotting readings on weather charts.

isobars are drawn. They link places of equal pressure. This shows up centres of high pressure (called anticyclones, or highs) and low pressure (called depressions, or lows).

The positions of any fronts,

or boundaries between air masses, are also marked. The completed synoptic chart now gives an accurate picture of what the weather was like in different places when the readings were taken.

Analysing The Weather

Now comes the difficult bit! The weather people have to try to predict, or forecast, what the future weather will be like. To do this, they study the synoptic chart they have just prepared and also the charts that came before it. This will give them a good idea of the way the weather is developing.

The forecasters use this information and also their experience of past weather to prepare another kind of weather map. This is called a prognostic chart. It shows what they think the weather conditions will be like at a certain time in the future. Using this chart, they then issue their forecast.

These days forecasting has been greatly improved by the use of computers. Weather computers are among the most powerful in the world. They can handle hundreds of millions of bits of data every second, and can make quite accurate forecasts for up to six days ahead.

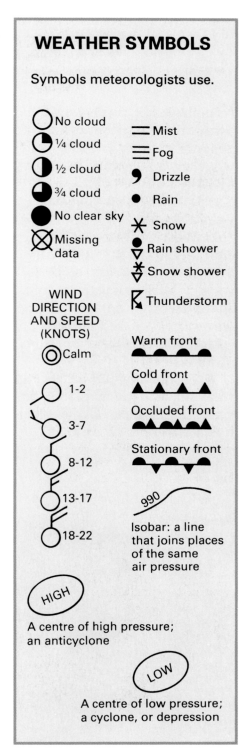

WEATHER SYMBOLS

Symbols meteorologists use.

No cloud
¼ cloud
½ cloud
¾ cloud
No clear sky
Missing data

Mist
Fog
Drizzle
Rain
Snow
Rain shower
Snow shower
Thunderstorm

WIND DIRECTION AND SPEED (KNOTS)
Calm
1-2
3-7
8-12
13-17
18-22

Warm front
Cold front
Occluded front
Stationary front

990
Isobar: a line that joins places of the same air pressure

HIGH
A centre of high pressure; an anticyclone

LOW
A centre of low pressure; a cyclone, or depression

WORLD WEATHER PATTERNS

In most parts of the world away from the Equator a gradual change in the weather takes place month by month. And this pattern of gradual change is repeated year after year.

In Western Europe, for example, January is usually cold and snowy; March is windy; April is showery; and so on. In other parts of the world the weather pattern throughout the year may be quite different.

We call the usual pattern of weather at a place during the year, the climate. Every place has a different climate. It depends on where exactly on the Earth it is.

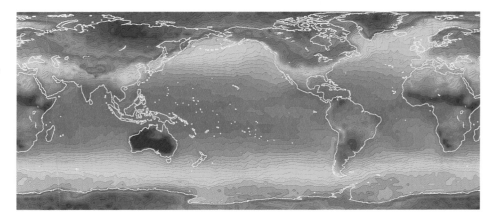

▲ **Temperature differences over the Earth in January. Reddest is warmest. This map used data from satellites.**

▼ **The world's main belts of prevailing winds. Winds are often light in the doldrums, near the Equator.**

Changing Temperatures

One of the main features of climate is temperature. The temperature varies all over the Earth because different parts of it receive different amounts of the Sun's heat (see page 8).

The unequal heating of the Earth's surface by the Sun sets up great movements of air in the atmosphere. These moving air masses have a marked effect on climate.

For example, around the Equator the air is heated and rises. It is full of moisture, which has evaporated from the hot oceans. As the warm, very moist air rises into the atmosphere, it cools. The moisture comes out of the air and falls as rain. This is the

Wind Belts

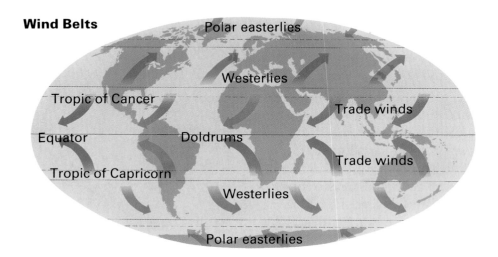

Polar easterlies
Westerlies
Tropic of Cancer
Trade winds
Equator   Doldrums
Trade winds
Tropic of Capricorn
Westerlies
Polar easterlies

reason for the heavy rainfall that occurs almost daily near the Equator.

Having shed its moisture, the air rising above the Equator is now dry. It spreads both north and south. Some of it sinks back to the surface at latitudes of about 30°. There it creates very dry conditions. This is the reason why many

north and due south but are deflected to the east or west. These prevailing winds have a marked effect on the world's climate.

The winds also set up movements, or currents, in the ocean waters. These currents affect climate as well. For example, north-west Europe enjoys quite a mild

Ocean Currents

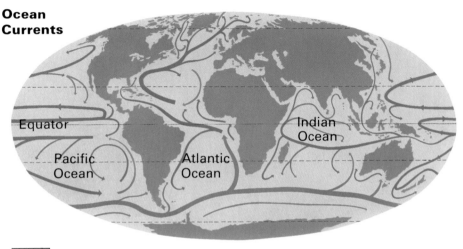

Equator

Indian Ocean

Pacific Ocean

Atlantic Ocean

Cold current

Warm current

▲ **The world's main ocean currents. They almost always follow the direction of the prevailing winds.**

deserts, such as the Sahara, are to be found near these latitudes.

Prevailing Winds
The descending air spreads out north and south over the surface, setting up winds. Because the Earth is rotating, these winds do not blow due

climate because the warm Gulf Stream passes nearby.

All coastal regions enjoy a much more moderate climate, called a maritime climate, compared with places in the middle of a continent, which have a continental climate.

Death Valley, in California (above), is one of the hottest places in the world. Temperatures of over 120°F (48.9°C) were recorded for 43 days in a row in July and August 1917. But the highest temperature ever recorded was 136.4°F (58°C) at al'Aziziyah, Libya, in September 1922.

Antarctica is the coldest place on Earth. It has an average yearly temperature of only −72°F (−57.8°C). The world's lowest temperature, −128.6°F (−89.2°C), was recorded at Vostok Station, in Antarctica, in July 1983.

WORLD CLIMATES

We can divide the world into a number of regions that have a similar climate: they have similar temperatures and rainfall throughout the year.

Tropical Climates
In the tropics, on either side of the Equator, the average monthly temperature is more than 65°F (18°C), and plenty of rain falls. In the dense rain forests rain falls almost daily. But in tropical grassland, or savanna regions, rain falls only during part of the year.

Dry Climates
However, in a dry, or desert climate little rain falls at any time. In very hot deserts rain may not fall for years at a time. Temperatures in the desert by day can soar up to 110°F (43°C) or more; at night they can drop to freezing.

Temperate Climates
The climate in temperate regions is neither too hot nor too cold. In warm temperate regions in the hottest month, the average temperature is

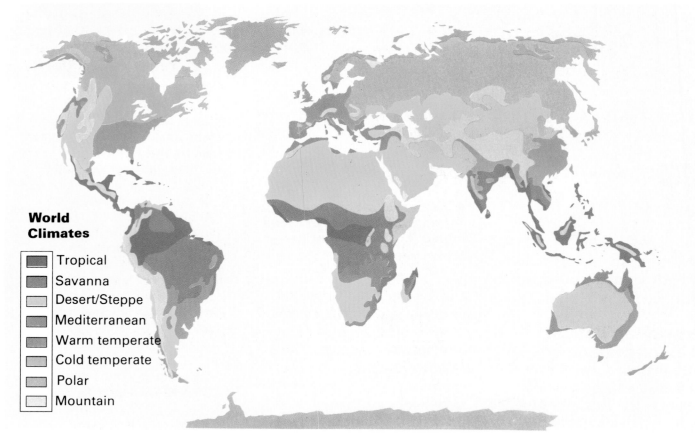

World Climates

- Tropical
- Savanna
- Desert/Steppe
- Mediterranean
- Warm temperate
- Cold temperate
- Polar
- Mountain

not above 65°F (18°C), and in the coldest month is not below 26°F (−3°C).

In cold temperate climates the average temperature in the coldest month is below 26°F (−3°C), and in the warmest month it is above 50°F (10°C). The region with this climate occupies a vast expanse of the Northern Hemisphere, across North America, Europe and Asia. It is often called the boreal region. Boreas was the Greek god of the north wind.

◄ **Tall Saguaro cacti growing in the Arizona Desert. The desert looks unusually green because rain has recently fallen.**

FACT FILE

● The tropics is a region on either side of the Equator, between two imaginary lines called the Tropic of Cancer (in the north) and the Tropic of Capricorn (in the south).
● A desert is described as a region in which an average of less than 10 inches (250mm) of rain falls in a year.

Cold Climates

The coldest parts of the world lie mainly around the North Pole, in the Arctic; and around the South Pole, in the Antarctic. These regions have a polar climate, in which the temperature never rises above 50°F (10°C) at any time. In winter temperatures drop below −60°F (−51°C).

An equally severe climate is found at the top of very high mountains, such as the Andes and Himalayas. It is called a mountain climate. Such a climate can occur anywhere, even near the Equator. This happens because the temperature falls the higher you go above sea level.

◄ **Adelie penguins in icy Antarctica. They cannot fly but are expert swimmers.**

WARM CLIMATES

The rain forests near the Equator enjoy the warmest and wettest climate on Earth. The high temperature and plentiful rainfall provide ideal conditions for plant life.

In the dense forests broad-leaved evergreen trees flower and fruit throughout the year. Their foliage forms a thick leafy canopy about 65 ft (20m) high. Lower down, shorter trees and shrubs form the understorey. The forest floor is quite dark because little sunlight can reach it.

▲ **A gorilla family feeding on the plentiful vegetation of the rain forest. The male 'silverback' leads the group.**

FACT FILE

● In the rain forests straddling the Equator the temperature stays about 77°F (25°C) throughout the year; and as much as 13 ft (4m) of rain falls every year.
● The Sahara Desert in Africa is by far the largest desert in the world; it covers an area nearly as big as the United States.
● No rain has fallen in the Atacama Desert in Chile for at least 400 years: it is the driest place in the world.

With plant food available all year, the forests support a rich variety of animal life: big cats like the leopard, and also elephants, gorillas, monkeys, birds and snakes.

Savanna and Prairie

The vast grasslands found in tropical regions also teem with wildlife. In the savanna regions of Africa there are great herds of grazing animals, such as impala and wildebeest. They are preyed upon by cheetahs and lions.

Plenty of rain falls in the savanna, but only in the wet season. No rain at all falls in the dry season, which can last up to six months.

Large areas of grassland are also found in the warm temperate regions. In North America they are called the prairie; in South America, the pampas; and in Asia, the steppe. These regions provide ideal conditions for grass and for crops like wheat.

▲ A tranquil landscape in western Europe, a warm temperate region. The grass is lush and grazing is good.

► The barren Kalahari Desert in southern Africa. Animals that stray into the desert do not survive for long.

Farmland And Forest

The grasslands are found in the middle of the continents. There is also plenty of rich farmland elsewhere in warm temperate regions.

These regions once used to be covered with forests, but

today few remain. They are made up mainly of broad-leaved trees, such as ash, oak and chestnut. These are deciduous trees, which lose their leaves in the autumn.

◄ Savanna country and wildlife in Kenya, East Africa. Life in the long dry season centres on the scattered waterholes.

Arid Desert

Deserts cover vast areas of the world. They are among the most forbidding regions on Earth. This is because of their very high temperatures and their lack of water.

But a surprising number of plants and animals live in the desert. They have found ways of coping with the deadly conditions. The best-known animal is the camel, the 'ship of the desert'. It can go for days without drinking, using water stored in its body. The best-known desert plant is the cactus, which can store water in its fleshy stems.

COOL CLIMATES

The Forest Belt

The cold temperate region occupies a huge belt across northern North America, Europe and Asia. There it is cold for much of the year. The summers are short.

The region is covered with thick forests. They are mainly conifer trees, such as fir, pine and spruce. These trees are evergreen and are specially adapted to stand up to the cold and snow. For example, they have needle-like leaves, which do not lose heat as readily as the broad leaves of most deciduous trees.

On The Tundra

North of the Arctic Circle conditions are far too harsh for big trees to survive. This region has a polar climate. Soil beneath the surface is permanently frozen, and is known as permafrost. Snow remains on the ground for much of the year.

This icy wilderness is called the tundra. Its typical plants include mosses, lichens and grasses. There are also a few shrubs. To survive, all these plants have to bud, flower and fruit very quickly because the growing season is so short.

The burst of summer growth on the tundra attracts plenty of wildlife. Herds of caribou migrate there from the dense evergreen forests.

▲ A scene at the northern boundary of the evergreen forest belt in North America. The trees are thinning going towards the tundra.

▶ Caribou find plenty of food on the tundra in summer. Then, for just a few weeks, the tundra bursts into colourful life and is abuzz with insects.

you pass through different climatic regions and different kinds of vegetation. Thick rain forest covers the lower slopes, and the climate is very hot and humid. Higher up, the climate becomes cooler. Trees give way to low shrubs, which in turn give way to a tundra-like region. Higher still comes the snow.

▼ A polar bear family out hunting on the ice floes near the North Pole. Seals provide much of their diet.

▲ In the severe climate in high mountain ranges, snow packs down to form glaciers, great 'rivers' of ice.

Geese flock there too in vast numbers to breed. Afterwards they fly south for the winter.

There is no tundra region in the Southern Hemisphere.

At The Poles

North of the tundra, nearer the North Pole, the climate gets even worse. The ground and much of the sea is always covered with ice.

At the other end of the Earth, the whole continent of Antarctica, around the South Pole, is always ice-covered.

Mountain Climates

Very cold conditions can also be found on high mountains, because the temperature falls as you climb upwards.

Even though Mt Kenya, in Africa, is near the Equator, snow is found at its summit. As you climb the mountain,

FACT FILE

● The North Pole is located in the frozen Arctic Ocean.
● Polar bears are found in the Arctic but not the Antarctic.
● Penguins are found in the Antarctic but not the Arctic.

CHANGING CLIMATES

THE OZONE HOLE

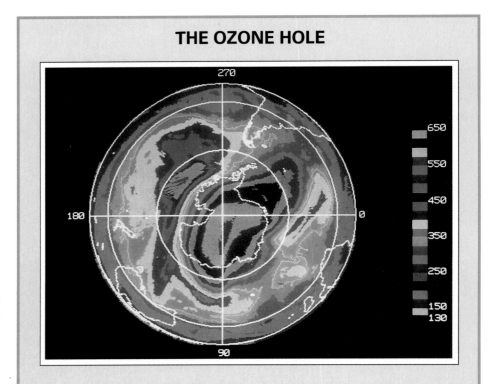

Today, most parts of Europe and North America enjoy quite a mild climate. But only about 10,000 years ago great sheets of ice covered much of the land. That was when the Earth was gripped in one of its many ice ages. At other times, the climate was much warmer than it is now.

These changes in climate came about naturally. Some

▼ **Burning the rain forests helps increase the greenhouse effect and destroys a precious natural resource.**

High in the atmosphere there is a layer of a gas called ozone, which is a kind of oxygen. It is important because it blocks dangerous rays from the Sun.

In 1982 scientists found that a region of the ozone layer over the Antarctic had become very thin. They called it the ozone hole. Since then such a hole has appeared over the Antarctic each year. The ozone layer has also been thinning over other regions.

Scientists believe that the hole is produced when chemicals called CFCs (chlorofluorocarbons) attack the ozone layer. CFCs get into the air from aerosol sprays, plastic foams and discarded refrigerators.

If the ozone layer thinned all over the world, it would let through more of the Sun's ultraviolet radiation. This would cause more cases of sunburn and skin cancer, and maybe damage our crops.

makes rivers and lakes too acid to support living things.

When they burn, fuels also give off heavy carbon dioxide gas. This, too, is building up in the atmosphere.

◀ **In the 1600s Europe was gripped in a 'Little ice age'. In London fairs were held on the frozen River Thames.**

does not seem much, but it would be enough to change the weather and climate over the whole world. For example, it would interfere with crop farming, and maybe cause

▼ **Power stations produce vast amounts of fumes. These cause acid rain and help increase the greenhouse effect.**

were caused by changes in the amount of heat coming from the Sun. Others came about because of the change in position of the continents. We call this continental drift.

Today, however, noticeable changes in the weather and climate are being brought about by human activities.

Burning Fuels

Many of the changes are taking place because we are burning far too much fuel: billions of tons of coal, oil and natural gas every year. When these fuels burn, they give off smoke, poisonous fumes and gases. These products are now building up in the air and causing serious pollution.

The gases include sulphur and nitrogen oxides. In the air they combine with moisture to form acids, which fall back to Earth when it rains. Acid rain damages trees and also

The Greenhouse Effect

The build-up of carbon dioxide is starting to turn the Earth's atmosphere into a kind of greenhouse. This greenhouse is trapping more of the Sun's heat and causing the climate to warm up.

Scientists fear that, in only about 50 years, temperatures around the world might rise by 9°F (5°C) or more. This

widespread crop failures and famine. It would cause ice to melt at the Poles. This would make the sea rise, and cause severe flooding in places.

But some scientists think that the greenhouse effect might be a good thing. They reckon that the global warming it is producing is stopping the Earth slipping into another ice age.

INDEX

PHOTOGRAPHIC CREDITS

Pictures are identified by page numbers and are keyed T (top), M (middle), B (bottom), R (right) and L (left). Ecoscene: 15, 21L, 24, 41B, 44B, 45B. Robin Kerrod: front cover (TR), 39T. Frank Lane Picture Agency: back cover, front cover (BR), 6, 7R, 12, 13, 14, 16, 17, 18, 19T, 21R, 23, 25B, 28, 29, 39B, 40, 41T, M, 42, 43. Mansell Collection: 45T. National Meteorological Library (Crown Copyright): 7L, 30, 31, 34, 35, 25T (© J. Roberts), 26 (© PPH Verschure), 32B (© ESA). NASA/Spacecharts: 8, 10, 19M, B, 27, 32T, 36, 37, 44T. NOAA: 33. ZEFA: front cover (L).